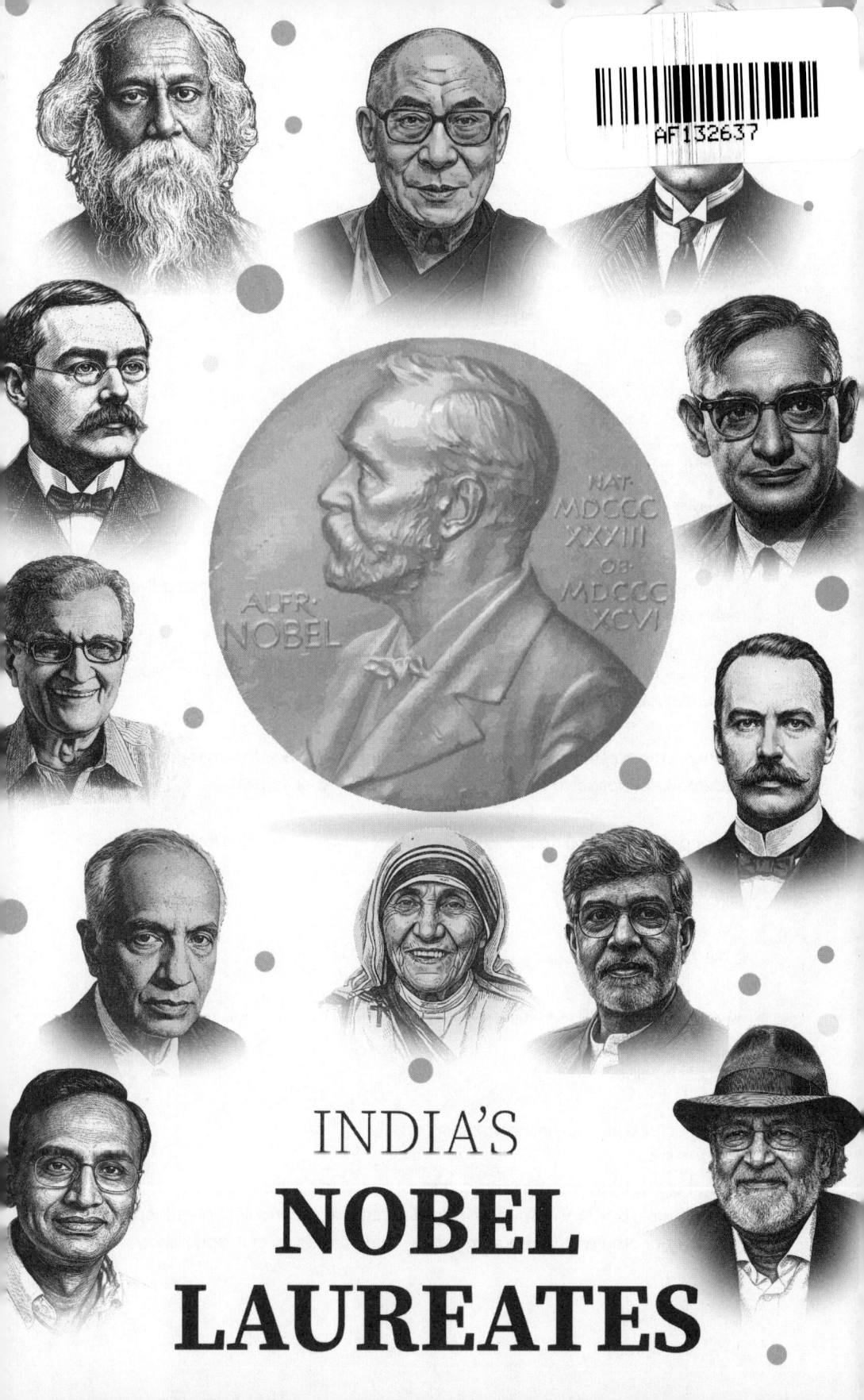

INDIA'S NOBEL LAUREATES

Published by Red Panda, an imprint of Westland Books, a division of Nasadiya Technologies Private Limited, in 2026

No. 269/2B, First Floor, 'Irai Arul', Vimalraj Street, Nethaji Nagar, Alapakkam Main Road, Maduravoyal, Chennai 600095

Westland, the Westland logo, Red Panda and the Red Panda logo are the trademarks of Nasadiya Technologies Private Limited, or its affiliates.

Text and illustrations © Nasadiya Technologies Private Limited, 2026

ISBN: 9789371971225

10 9 8 7 6 5 4 3 2 1

Book design by Pratik M. Kalekar

All rights reserved

Printed at Parksons Graphics Pvt. Ltd

No part of this book may be reproduced, or stored in a retrieval system, or transmitted in any form or by any means, electronic, mechanical, photocopying, recording, or otherwise, without express written permission of the publisher.

CONTENTS

Born in India, Honoured by the World
Rabindranath Tagore 8
C. V. Raman 18
Mother Teresa 26
Amartya Sen 34
Kailash Satyarthi 42

Indian Roots, Global Impact
Har Gobind Khorana 52
Subrahmanyan Chandrasekhar 60
Venkatraman Ramakrishnan 68
V. S. Naipaul 76

Nobel Work on Indian Soil
Ronald Ross 84
Rudyard Kipling 92

Laureates Who Call India Home
14th Dalai Lama 100

Born in India, Honoured by the World

Laureates who carried an Indian passport and changed the world with their brilliance, compassion and courage.

Rabindranath Tagore

Born: 7 May 1861, Calcutta, Bengal Presidency, British India

Nobel Prize: Literature, 1913

Famous For: *Gitanjali* (Song Offerings), India's national anthem and numerous other works of poetry

Died: 7 August 1941, Calcutta, Bengal Presidency, British India

The Boy Who Loved Stories

Long ago, in the bustling city of Calcutta, there lived a little boy named Rabindranath. He was born into the illustrious Tagore family, who were known throughout Bengal for their love of art, music and learning. But young Rabindranath was quite different from children his age.

While other boys played with toys or chased one another through courtyards, Rabindranath sat listening to adults discuss literature and philosophy. The Tagore household was always filled with visitors—poets, musicians, writers and thinkers who would gather to share their ideas and create wonderful works of art.

Rabindranath's father, Debendranath Tagore, was a patron of art and culture who believed in both Indian traditions and modern ideas. His mother, Sarada Devi, filled the house with warmth and love. Though she died when Rabindranath was quite young, her gentle spirit stayed with him throughout his life.

Throughout his childhood, he found himself at odds with the schools of his time. The rigid Victorian schools had children sitting still for hours, mindlessly memorising and chanting their lessons. Young Rabindranath's restless mind, dancing with stories and images, felt caged in those suffocating classrooms. Instead, he preferred to roam around his family's gardens, watching the birds, listening to the wind in the trees and making up stories and poems in his head.

> **Did you know?**
>
> *Young Rabindranath once wrote, 'I do not remember what I was taught, but I remember what I loved.'*

A Young Poet Discovers His Voice

The first signs of Rabindranath's gift as a poet appeared when he was just eight years old. He wrote his very first poem inspired by Bernardin de Saint-Pierre's French novel *Paul et Virginie*. It wasn't very long, but it showed that even as a child, he had a special gift for putting beautiful thoughts into words.

As he grew older, Rabindranath's love for writing grew stronger and stronger. By the time he was sixteen, he had already published his first book of poems titled *Kabi Kahini*. Can you imagine writing a whole book of poetry whilst you're still at school?

But Rabindranath didn't just write in Bengali, his mother tongue. He also learned English and began translating his own works. This was quite unusual at that time, as most Indian writers only wrote in their mother-tongue or local languages.

His family supported his passion completely. They understood that Rabindranath was meant to be a poet, not to follow the conventional paths of commerce or law like many young men of his time. They gave him the freedom to travel, to learn and to write about the world around him. Since then, Rabindranath grew into one of the most accomplished and beloved poets the world has ever known. What made him truly special was his ability to speak to both the heart and the mind, weaving together deep philosophical ideas with imagery so beautiful it felt like music.

The Teacher Who Built a Dream School

Rabindranath believed that children should learn in a happy, natural environment rather than in stuffy classrooms. In 1901, he started a very special school called Santiniketan, which means 'abode of peace' in Bengali.

At Santiniketan, children didn't have to sit in rows memorising facts. Instead, they learned under trees, in gardens and by exploring nature. They studied art, music and poetry alongside mathematics and science. Rabindranath wanted his students to become complete human beings, not just clever at passing examinations.

The school welcomed children from all over India and even from other countries. Rich and poor children learned together, and everyone was treated equally. This was quite revolutionary at a time when society was divided by class and caste.

Later, Santiniketan grew into Visva-Bharati University, which still exists today. Students from around the world come to study there, continuing Rabindranath's dream of bringing different cultures together through education.

Songs, Stories and the Nobel Prize

Rabindranath wrote over 2,000 songs during his lifetime! These weren't just any songs—they were beautiful compositions that combined poetry with melody. Many of his songs are still sung today, and two of them became national anthems: *Jana Gana Mana* for India and *Amar Sonar Bangla* for Bangladesh.

But it was his poetry that made him famous throughout the

world. In 1910, he wrote a collection of poems called *Gitanjali*, which means 'song offerings'. These were spiritual poems that spoke about love, nature and the connection between humans and God.

> *'Let my thoughts come to you, when I am gone, like*
> *the afterglow of sunset at the margin*
> *of starry silence.'*

When Rabindranath translated *Gitanjali* into English, it caught the attention of the Western literary world. The famous Irish poet W.B. Yeats read the poems and was so moved by them that he wrote a glowing introduction to the book. Soon, people all over Europe and America were reading and loving Rabindranath's poetry.

In 1913, Rabindranath won the Nobel Prize for Literature, becoming the first non-European to receive this honour. While the achievement brought immense pride to India and Asia, Rabindranath himself remained characteristically humble, viewing the award as a bridge between cultures rather than a personal triumph.

Did you know?

Tagore's Nobel Medal and citation were stolen in 2004 from Santiniketan. Later, replicas were gifted to India by the Swedish Academy.

The Artist Who Never Stopped Learning

Even though Rabindranath was already famous as a poet, he was always trying to learn something new. When he was sixty years old, he decided to try his hand at painting! Most people thought he was too old to learn a new skill, but Rabindranath proved them wrong.

His paintings were quite different from traditional Indian art. They were bold, colourful and showed his unique way of seeing and expressing the world. Art galleries in many countries displayed his paintings, and people were amazed that the same person could be talented at both writing and visual art. He was a versatile genius who kept expanding his artistic boundaries. He moved from poetry to novels, plays, music composition and philosophical writing, always seeking new ways to express his ideas.

Rabindranath also loved to travel. He visited countries like Japan, China, England, America and Russia, meeting people from different cultures and learning about their ways of life. These experiences made his writing richer and helped him understand that all humans, regardless of where they come from, share similar hopes and dreams.

A Voice for Freedom and Peace

Although Tagore was not involved in political struggles in the same way as Mahatma Gandhi, he stood firm in his beliefs. In 1919, after the Jallianwala Bagh massacre, in which hundreds of peaceful Indian protestors were killed by British troops, Tagore renounced his knighthood and returned the British title of 'Sir' in protest.

He believed in non-violence, mutual respect and the dignity of all people. He also warned against narrow nationalism. He said true freedom meant not just breaking chains but also opening minds.

He wrote many poems and songs that inspired people to love their country and work towards independence. His song *Jana Gana Mana* filled people's hearts with pride and hope for a free India.

> *'The highest education is that which does not merely give us information but makes our life in*

harmony with all existence.'

Rabindranath also believed in bringing people together rather than dividing them. He thought that different countries and cultures should learn from each other instead of fighting. This message of universal brotherhood made him respected not just in India but all over the world.

His famous poem *Chitto Jetha Bhoyshunyo*, written in Bengali and later translated by Tagore himself into English as *Where the Mind is Without Fear,* speaks of this dream.

This poem was included in his Nobel-winning collection *Gitanjali*, and it continues to inspire generations with its vision of a free and fearless India.

The Legacy That Lives On

Rabindranath Tagore passed away in 1941, but his influence continues to this day. His poems are still read by millions of people; his songs are sung in schools and concerts and his ideas about education continue to inspire teachers around the world.

Santiniketan, the school he founded, remains a special place where students from different countries come to study art, music, literature and culture together. The university continues to follow his vision of learning through joy and creativity rather than fear and competition.

In India, Rabindranath is lovingly called 'Gurudev', which means 'great teacher'. This title shows how much people respect him not just as a writer but as someone who taught important lessons about life, love and human dignity.

His birthday is celebrated as Rabindra Jayanti in West Bengal and Bangladesh. On this day, people organise cultural programmes, recite his poetry and sing his songs to remember this great man.

> *'Let my thoughts come to you, when I am gone, like the afterglow of sunset at the margin of starry silence.'*

Today, when you sing the Indian national anthem *Jana Gana Mana*, remember that these stirring words were written by a poet who believed in the power of education, the beauty of art and the importance of treating all people with love and respect. Rabindranath Tagore showed the world that India had much to offer in terms of wisdom, creativity and spiritual insight.

His life teaches us that we should never stop learning, never stop creating and never stop believing in the goodness of humanity. Just like the young boy who preferred poetry to playtime, we too can follow our dreams and make the world a more beautiful place through our talents and kindness.

∎

C. V. Raman

 Born: 7 November 1888, Tiruchirappalli (Trichinopoly), Madras Presidency, British India

 Nobel Prize: Physics, 1930

 Famous For: Discovering the Raman Effect, which explains how light behaves when it passes through different substances

 Died: 21 November 1970, Bangalore

A Boy Who Questioned Everything

Chandrasekhara Venkata Raman was born on 7 November 1888 in the small town of Tiruchirappalli, in present-day Tamil Nadu. His father, Chandrasekhara Iyer, was a college lecturer in mathematics and physics. Their home was filled with books, questions and conversations about numbers, nature and the wonders of the world.

Raman was a quiet and thoughtful child. While others played outside, He would slip into his father's study and lose himself for hours, poring through enormous volumes of books on everything from Buddhism to geometry. His mind was always full of questions. Why does the sky look blue? Why does water sparkle in sunlight? Why does glass shine in the dark? He did not simply ask and forget. He followed his questions with experiments, using whatever he had at home–bits of glass, bottles, string and sunlight.

'Ask the right questions, and nature will open the doors to her deepest secrets.'

Even though his family did not have much money, they had a rich atmosphere of learning. His father shared his love of science and mathematics with him, while his mother encouraged him to enjoy music, poetry and stories. He was fascinated by classical

Indian percussion instruments like the tabla and mridangam, a passion he would carry with him throughout his life. This mix of logic and creativity shaped Raman's curious and fearless mind.

By the age of eleven, Raman had already completed school and entered college. He was the youngest in his class at Presidency College in Madras. Though he was small and quiet, he stood out because of his brilliant mind. He studied physics and won gold medals in every subject. Yet what set him apart was not just his academic success; it was his genuine curiosity about how things worked. He was driven by an urge not just learn or memorise, but to discover.

From a Quiet Office to a Brilliant Discovery

Even though Raman was passionate about science, there were very few opportunities to work as a full-time scientist in India at that time. Most scientific research was done by Europeans or in British-run institutes. So in 1907, after topping his university exams, Raman joined the Indian Finance Service at the age of 19. He was posted to Calcutta as an Assistant Accountant General, a well-paid and respected government job. Even though it provided a secure career and a decent income, the hectic accounting job felt suffocating to him. He realised that nothing could excite him like science. Only when he was experimenting or observing did he truly feel alive.

> *'I feel it is unnatural for a scientist to not wonder about the everyday phenomena that surround us.'*

That is when he got acquainted with some scientists from the Indian Association for the Cultivation of Science (IACS), Calcutta, the first research institute founded in India. Soon, he received permission to research at IACS during his spare time. By day, he sat at his desk checking numbers and files. But as soon as his office work was over, he walked across the city to the IACS campus. There, in his laboratory, Raman carried out his experiments with energy and enthusiasm.

He did not have expensive machines or shiny new instruments. He would work late into the night, studying how light passed through different materials, how it bent and scattered and what secrets it might reveal.

In 1921, Raman took a ship to Europe for a scientific tour. On his way back to India, he stood on the deck and stared at the Mediterranean Sea. The water looked deep blue. Most people believed it was just the reflection of the sky. But Raman was not convinced. The colour seemed too rich and mysterious. He felt certain that something more was happening. That simple moment sparked one of the most important discoveries in modern science.

Did you know?

Raman's laboratory had no advanced equipment. He used sunlight, a black cloth and glass containers to make his discovery—proving that big ideas do not always need big machines.

Back in Calcutta, Raman began a series of experiments with his trusted colleague, K. S. Krishnan. Together, they studied how light behaved when it passed through different liquids. On 28 February 1928, after many careful trials, they observed something amazing. A small part of the light changed colour after passing through a liquid. This meant that light was not just bouncing off; it was interacting with the liquid particles and undergoing changes.

This discovery became known as the Raman Effect, and it changed the way scientists understood light and matter. It showed that light could reveal the inner structure of molecules. It opened a new field in science called Raman spectroscopy, which became a powerful tool in physics, chemistry and medicine.

A Flash of Light on the Global Stage

When Raman shared his discovery with the world, scientists everywhere took notice. Until then, no one had seen this kind of light scattering in such a clear and simple way. His results were not only accurate, they were elegant. They were researched with limited resources, but great intelligence.

In 1930, the Royal Swedish Academy of Sciences awarded C. V. Raman the Nobel Prize in Physics. He was the first Asian and the first person of colour to win a Nobel Prize in any science. He received the honour 'for his work on the scattering of light and for the discovery of the effect named after him'.

'The essence of science is independent thinking, hard work and not equipment.'

When he got the news of the prize, Raman was overjoyed. It was not just a personal victory. It showed the world that Indian science had a voice, a mind and a future. At the Nobel ceremony in Stockholm, Raman gave a powerful lecture, speaking with passion about his love for science and his belief in curiosity and courage.

> **Did you know?**
>
> *Raman refused to travel on a British ship to Sweden. Instead, he sailed on an Indian vessel as a quiet statement of pride in his identity.*

Raman's Nobel win became a symbol of hope for millions of Indians living under British rule. At a time when India was fighting for freedom, his success proved that Indian minds could reach the highest peaks of global achievement.

Light Beyond the Lab: The Enduring Spark of C. V. Raman

After winning the Nobel Prize, Raman did not rest. He continued to teach, research and inspire others. In 1933, he became the first Indian director of the Indian Institute of Science (IISc) in Bangalore. There, he trained and encouraged a new generation of Indian scientists.

In 1948, a year after India became independent, Raman founded the Raman Research Institute in Bangalore. He wanted it to be a place where bright minds could work freely and explore without fear. He believed that science should grow in India with confidence and independence.

'The true spirit of science is to ask questions and never be afraid of the answers.'

Raman believed that scientific greatness did not depend on money or foreign degrees. What mattered most was honesty, imagination and perseverance.

Did you know?

Although he had been knighted by the British in 1929, Raman later refused all British honours after Independence. He chose instead to serve India with dignity and pride.

Throughout his life, Raman stayed true to his values. He stood up for science, for education and for the power of ideas.

Even in his later years, he continued to work at the lab and guide young researchers.

C. V. Raman passed away on 21 November 1970. But his legacy is alive in classrooms, laboratories, and space missions across the world. His discovery, the Raman Effect, is now used in Raman spectroscopy, a technique that helps scientists examine the structure of materials. It is used in fields as wide-ranging as medicine, chemistry, art conservation, environmental science and even space exploration.

Every year on 28 February, India celebrates National Science Day to mark the day C.V. Raman made his groundbreaking discovery. Schools and colleges across the country hold science fairs, exhibitions, quizzes and fun experiments. It's a day to honour Raman's spirit of curiosity and to inspire children to ask questions, explore the world around them and dream like scientists.

C. V. Raman's greatest contribution may not have been just a scientific theory, but a message: that every curious child, no matter where they come from, has the power to change the world.

■

Mother Teresa

 Born: 26 August 1910, Skopje (then part of the Ottoman Empire, now North Macedonia)

 Nobel Prize: Peace, 1979

 Famous For: Helping the poorest of the poor in India and founding the Missionaries of Charity

 Died: 5 September 1997, Kolkata

A Heart Born to Serve

Agnes Gonxha Bojaxhiu was born in a small city called Skopje, the bustling market town nestled in the heart of the Balkans. Her family was Albanian, and they were devout Catholics. From a young age, little Agnes learned what her wealthy family believed: that helping others wasn't optional, it was essential. She would often share her food, visit the sick with her mother and help anyone in need.

Her father, Nikollë, was a merchant deeply involved in Albanian politics—until his sudden death when Agnes was just eight years old. Overnight, everything changed. Her mother, Drana, a deeply religious housewife, took up sewing and embroidering to support her children. Through long hours of needlework and prayer, she kept the family together, teaching Agnes that faith and determination could carry you through anything.

'If you cannot feed a hundred people, then feed just one.'

At 12, Agnes felt something stir deep inside her—a calling. She wanted to become a nun and help others through the Church. Her decision solidified during a pilgrimage to the shrine of the Black Madonna of Vitina-Letnice in Kosovo, a place she had returned to again and again throughout her youth. By the time she turned

18, she had made a big decision. She left her family and friends behind to join the Sisters of Loreto, a congregation of women in Ireland in 1928. There, she took on a new name, Sister Teresa, after Saint Thérèse of Lisieux, the patron saint of missionaries.

> **Did you know?**
>
> *Agnes was fascinated by stories of missionaries in far-off lands. India, in particular, held a special place in her heart.*

Soon, she was sent to India to begin her new life. She travelled to the bustling city of Calcutta (now Kolkata), where she became a teacher at St Mary's High School. The young Sister Teresa believed that education was one way to help the poor rise above hardship. But it wouldn't be long before her journey took an even more powerful turn.

Beyond the Convent Walls: The Turning Point in Calcutta

For nearly 20 years, Sister Teresa lived within the calm walls of the convent, teaching girls and guiding them with faith. But outside those walls, life in Calcutta was anything but calm. The city, filled with rickshaws, temples and crowds, was also marked by poverty, disease and sorrow.

In 1946, during a train journey to the Himalayan foothills, Sister Teresa experienced something life-changing. She described it as 'a call within a call'. She felt God wanted her not to remain in the convent but to go out and live among the poor.

> *'I had to leave the convent and help the poor while living among them. It was an order.'*

Noble as her mission was, the beginning proved harder than she'd imagined. She had no money, no shelter and no plan. But with courage in her heart, she stepped out onto the streets of Calcutta. She began by helping one person at a time—washing wounds, offering comfort or providing meals.

To truly understand and connect with those she served, she learned Bengali and trained in basic medical care. In 1948, she officially became an Indian citizen. The country she had come to love was now her home.

In 1950, she founded a new religious order called the Missionaries of Charity. Its mission was simple: to care for 'the hungry, the naked, the homeless, the crippled, the blind, the lepers, all those people who feel unwanted, unloved, uncared for throughout society'.

At first, it was just her. Then a few of her former students joined her. Slowly, word spread. Donations trickled in. More volunteers arrived. The Missionaries of Charity grew into a sisterhood of love.

Did you know?

The missionary's first shelter was a small, abandoned building where they took in people dying on the streets, offering them dignity and care in their final days.

Mother Teresa always believed that even the smallest act of kindness could shine like a candle in the dark.

A Prize for Peace: The World Notices a Humble Nun

By the 1970s, Mother Teresa was no longer just a figure in the streets of Calcutta. Her work had touched hearts across the globe. Photos of her bent over the sick, holding hands with lepers and comforting the dying were printed in newspapers and magazines worldwide. Her message stood out in a world of noise and complexity: love in action. She did not campaign or debate. Her tools were a worn white sari with a blue border, a rosary in hand and boundless compassion.

Her deep humility caught the world's attention. In 1971, she received the Pope John XXIII Peace Prize. In 1972, she was awarded the Jawaharlal Nehru Award for International Understanding by the Indian government. Still, she remained uninterested in personal glory. She often said that she was 'just a pencil in God's hand.'

Then in 1979, the Nobel Committee awarded her the Nobel Peace Prize for her unwavering work with the poor, the dying and the forgotten. Her Missionaries of Charity had grown from a small order in Kolkata to an international organisation, running centres in more than 30 countries. Yet, she continued to live and dress simply. When asked how people could help bring peace to the world, she responded, 'Go home and love your family.'

> *'Not all of us can do great things. But we can do small things with great love.'*

At the Nobel ceremony in Oslo, Mother Teresa chose to wear her usual simple cotton sari. Instead of attending the traditional grand banquet, she requested that the $192,000 prize money be used to feed and shelter the poor in India.

Her refusal to let fame distract her became her greatest strength. While awards poured in—including the Bharat Ratna in 1980 and the United States Presidential Medal of Freedom in 1985—she never allowed the spotlight to dim her true purpose.

Her travels increased after the Nobel win. She visited war zones, disaster areas and places where others feared to go. In Beirut, Lebanon, she crossed battle lines during a ceasefire to rescue thirty-seven children trapped in a hospital. She opened homes for AIDS patients in New York and San Francisco at a time when fear and misinformation about the disease ran high.

By the early 1980s, the Missionaries of Charity had over 3,000 members and growing numbers of lay volunteers. Yet, Mother Teresa continued to sweep the floors in her homes and bathe the sick with her own hands. She never allowed her identity to shift from a servant of God's will to a celebrity.

Her life reminded the world that peace does not begin at summits or behind podiums. It begins in homes, in kind words, in giving without expecting and in recognising the dignity of even the most broken among us.

Did you know?

Mother Teresa's Nobel Peace Prize acceptance speech was delivered entirely without notes. She spoke from memory and from the heart.

The Final Journey: Love Without Limits

Even after receiving the Nobel Prize, Mother Teresa didn't slow down. She continued to open homes, orphanages and hospices in dozens of countries. From Ethiopia to Venezuela, from New York to Albania, her mission spread like ripples from a single drop of water.

By the 1990s, the Missionaries of Charity had over 4,000 sisters and thousands of volunteers. Yet, Mother Teresa still believed her greatest work happened in silence, in one-to-one moments of care.

In her final years, her health began to fade. She suffered from heart problems and even stepped down briefly from leading her order. But her spirit remained strong. She was seen praying with the dying, speaking softly to children and guiding her sisters with warmth.

> *'I am a little pencil in the hand of a writing God, who is sending a love letter to the world.'*

Mother Teresa died on 5 September 1997 in Kolkata. The whole world mourned. Her funeral was held with full state honours and attended by kings, queens, presidents, religious leaders and thousands of ordinary people whose lives she had touched. She lay in repose at St Thomas's Church before her body was taken in a grand procession to the headquarters of the Missionaries of Charity.

Pope John Paul II fast-tracked her canonisation. Normally, sainthood takes decades, but she was beatified in 2003 and declared Saint Teresa of Calcutta in 2016.

Today, her legacy lives on. Her order continues to care for the forgotten and the suffering in over 130 countries. Schools, hospitals, shelters and community kitchens carry her mission forward.

Did you know?

Mother Teresa's sari, the simple white cloth with blue borders, is now recognised as a symbol of compassion.

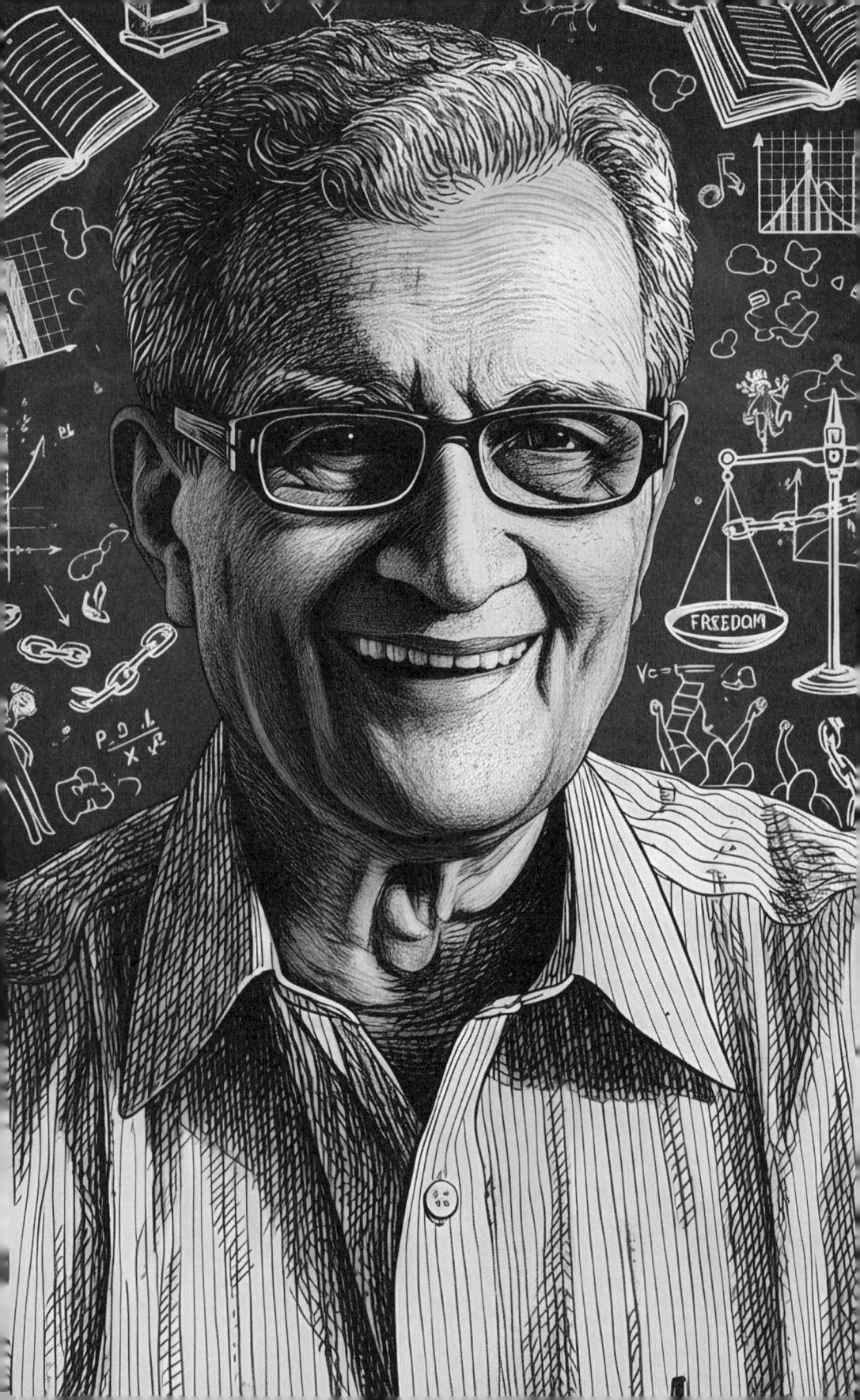

Amartya Sen

Born: 3 November 1933, Santiniketan, West Bengal, India

Nobel Prize: Economic Sciences, 1979

Famous For: Reshaping how the world understands poverty, welfare and human development.

The Argumentative Economist

Amartya Sen was born in 1933 in the Santiniketan campus, founded by Rabindranath Tagore. Raised in an environment that nurtured curiosity and openness, Sen's early years were shaped by both scholarly values and the rich cultural heritage of Bengal. His father, Ashutosh Sen, was a professor of chemistry, and his mother, Amita Sen, had deep interests in literature and music.

From the very beginning, Amartya was immersed in a world where books, ideas and philosophical discussions were a daily affair. He was named 'Amartya' by Tagore himself, which means 'immortal' in Sanskrit. The name would prove to be prophetic, as his ideas would go on to reshape how the world thinks about poverty, inequality and justice.

As a child, he witnessed the Bengal Famine of 1943. Though he was not personally affected, seeing people die of starvation while food was available elsewhere in the region left a lasting impression on him. This real-life contradiction between plenty and poverty planted the seeds for what would become his revolutionary work on entitlement theory.

'The roots of the problems of hunger are not found in food production but in the way in which access to food is governed.'

After finishing school at Santiniketan, Amartya moved on to Presidency College in Kolkata where he studied economics and mathematics. He stood out not only for his academic brilliance but also for his keen sense of justice. At eighteen, his life was derailed by a devastating diagnosis of oral cancer. The Kolkata hospital where he was treated had few resources, and the doctors gave him a grim verdict—just a 15 percent chance of living past five years. He was treated at a hospital in Kolkata with limited resources, and his survival influenced his later work on healthcare inequality. But against all odds, he pulled through. Later, he moved to Trinity College, Cambridge to get a second BA degree in Economics. He thrived at Cambridge, eventually rising to become president of the Cambridge Majlis, a debating and cultural society that brought together South Asian students. It was during his time there that he began to develop his life's most impactful ideas.

Shaping Global Thinking: The Rise of a New Economic Voice

In the 1950s and 60s, Amartya's intellectual journey took off as he started teaching and researching at some of the world's top universities, including the University of Delhi, London School of Economics, Oxford and Harvard.

Sen's groundbreaking work on social choice theory challenged traditional economics that focused only on utility and wealth. Instead, he asked, 'What can people actually do with what they have?' He focused on the idea of capabilities, arguing that true development means giving people the freedom to lead lives they have reason to value.

His book Poverty and Famines (1981) presented a bold idea: famines do not necessarily occur due to a lack of food, but due to a lack of access. Through detailed studies, he showed how markets, wages and political inaction can block people from obtaining food, even when there is enough to go around. This theory influenced both policy and humanitarian work around the globe.

> **Did you know?**
>
> *Sen was the first Asian to head an Oxbridge college when he became Master of Trinity College, Cambridge, in 1998.*

He also worked closely with the United Nations and the World Bank, often advocating for a broader approach to development that includes healthcare, education and gender equity. With philosopher Martha Nussbaum, he developed the this idea further, especially in terms of gender justice and disability rights.

In 1999, he published Development as Freedom, a book that reached beyond academic circles and found a wide readership. It argued that real progress must be measured not just in GDP, but in what freedoms people actually enjoy: access to education, the right to vote, basic healthcare and the ability to speak without fear.

'Development has to be more than just the accumulation of wealth. It is about expanding human freedoms.'

He continued teaching and researching, influencing not only economists, but also political scientists, philosophers and social workers. By now, he had become one of the most respected intellectuals in the world.

The Nobel Moment: Recognition on the World Stage

By the late 1990s, Amartya Sen's work had touched lives across disciplines and continents. In 1998, he was awarded the Nobel

Prize in Economic Sciences for his contributions to welfare economics and his work on the causes of famine, social choice and poverty.

When asked about the award, Amartya remained characteristically modest. He said the prize recognised a field of economics that focused on real-world problems. He also noted that his mother, then in her 90s, was more thrilled than he was. In his Nobel acceptance speech, he stressed that development should focus on enhancing human lives, especially for the most vulnerable

> *'The Nobel Prize was not just about me. It was about the importance of addressing poverty and inequality.'*

He also used the attention from the Nobel to further his advocacy. He encouraged governments to invest in public health, empower women and design policies that take local contexts into account. His work inspired the creation of the Human Development Index (HDI) by the United Nations, which evaluates countries based on health, education and income rather than just GDP.

> **Did you know?**
>
> *When Sen won the Nobel Prize, sales of his academic books surged, and Development as Freedom became a bestseller.*

After the award, he travelled extensively, giving lectures and working with development agencies.

A Legacy of Reason: Sen's Life After the Nobel

Even after the Nobel Prize, Amartya Sen continued to teach, write and speak about the deeper meaning of justice and development.

He returned to Harvard as a professor and later taught at Nalanda University in India, helping to revive the ancient centre of learning.

He published *The Idea of Justice* in 2009, a major philosophical work where he compared Western and Eastern ideas of fairness. Instead of imagining a perfectly just society, Sen argued that we should focus on reducing injustice in real-world situations.

> *'Justice is not about designing the ideal society, but about removing the suffering and injustice we see around us.'*

Sen also became increasingly involved in public debates in India. He spoke out on issues such as freedom of speech, minority rights and secularism. He argued that India must adhere to its pluralistic and democratic identity. Always measured, never dramatic, his voice stood as a reminder that democracy requires reason, dialogue and compassion.

Did you know?

In 2010, Sen was awarded the Bharat Ratna, India's highest civilian honour.

His later years were also marked by collaborations with global thinkers on climate change, education and public policy. Sen believed that facing future challenges like pandemics, environmental collapse and digital inequality required ethical reasoning and collective action.

He remains a guiding light for younger economists and philosophers. Universities around the world hold conferences on his work, and his writings continued to influence policy at the highest levels.

Today, Amartya Sen stands as one of the few public intellectuals whose ideas have genuinely improved millions of lives. His life's work has not only enriched economics but has also helped create a more compassionate and thoughtful world.

■

Kailash Satyarthi

 Born: 11 January 1954, Vidisha, Madhya Pradesh,

 Nobel Prize: Peace, 2014
(shared with Malala Yousafzai)

 Famous For: Rescuing children from bonded labour and child slavery

A Mission for Childhood

Kailash Satyarthi was born on 11 January 1954 in the quiet town of Vidisha, Madhya Pradesh. His family lived modestly. His father was a police constable and his mother a homemaker. They had little money, but education was the one thing they refused to compromise on. His mother's compassion shaped him deeply—her example of helping others without hesitation became the foundation of who he would become. Growing up in a mixed neighbourhood where Hindus and Muslims lived side by side, young Kailash learned Urdu from the local mosque's maulvi at age four, adding it to the Hindi and English he was picking up at school.

Every morning, young Kailash would walk to school with freshly polished shoes, neatly combed hair and a satchel full of books. But on the way, he often passed children who were not going to school at all. Some were sweeping the floor of sweet shops, some carrying stacks of plates at dhabas and others lifting bricks in construction yards.

One day, just six years old, he turned to his teacher and asked, 'Why don't these children go to school like me?'

His teacher gave an him a discomforting about poverty, about how some children had other obligations. But even then, Kailash knew something was wrong. Why should one child carry books while another carried burdens?

That question never left him.

> **Did you know?**
>
> *Kailash dropped his caste-identifying surname 'Sharma' and adopted the name 'Satyarthi', which means 'seeker of truth'.*

His family hoped he would become an engineer, and he followed that path at first. He studied electrical engineering and began teaching at a college in Bhopal. His life was comfortable, his future safe. But within him, that old question still burned. The children who had been pushed to the margins had not disappeared. Neither had his sense of injustice.

One afternoon, after seeing a boy working outside a school he could never enter, Kailash decided that enough was enough. He resigned from his job and began a journey unlike any other.

From Classroom to Rescue Missions

After giving up his teaching career in 1980, he setup a movement to fight for children no one else was fighting for. He called his movement Bachpan Bachao Andolan—Save Childhood Movement. Its goal was simple but enormous: to end child labour and give every child the right to a childhood.

He started small, visiting factories, brick kilns and stone quarries. What he found was heartbreaking. Children as young as five were working in filthy, dangerous conditions, often beaten or locked away, without any hope of escape. Kailash began planning rescue missions.

These missions were dangerous. Sometimes he had to sneak in at night. Sometimes he faced mobs or violent owners. He was beaten multiple times. Once, during a rescue in Uttar Pradesh, he was hospitalised after a brutal attack. Yet, he pressed on.

> *'Child slavery is a crime against humanity.*
> *Humanity itself is at stake here.'*

Alongside rescuing children, Kailash and his team ensured they had a place to heal. He helped build rehabilitation centres and schools where children could play, study and have a new beginning. His model became a blueprint—not just for India, but for other countries as well.

By the early 1990s, he was no longer just rescuing children— he was changing laws. Kailash worked with lawmakers to push for stricter rules against bonded labour and trafficking. His voice echoed not just in villages and cities, but in courtrooms and parliaments as well.

Did you know?

One of his most successful campaigns, the Global March Against Child Labour in 1998, crossed over 100 countries and led to the adoption of United Nations' ILO Convention 182 on the Worst Forms of Child Labour.

A Nobel Moment for Every Child

On 10 October 2014, the Nobel Committee in Oslo made a historic announcement. The Nobel Peace Prize would be jointly awarded to Kailash Satyarthi and Malala Yousafzai, the young Pakistani activist for girls' education. It was a powerful statement —one from India, one from Pakistan. One who saved children from labour, and one who fought for their right to education.

Kailash was in the middle of a rescue mission when he got the call announcing the news. At first, he thought it was a prank. But as the calls kept coming, reality sank in. 'I had dedicated my life to the cause of children. I never imagined that the world would recognise it in this way,' he said later.

In December that year, Kailash stood on the stage in Oslo, shoulder to shoulder with Malala. In his speech, he spoke not just of rights, but of compassion.

'Every single child matters. Every single childhood stolen is a shame on us all. We must not look away.'

Instead of accepting the spotlight for himself, he reminded the world of those still await for rescue. The Nobel Prize brought global attention to a topic often buried in silence. News outlets, governments and schools began discussing child labour with a new urgency.

> **Did you know?**
>
> *Kailash Satyarthi became the first Indian-born Nobel Peace Prize winner after Mother Teresa.*

Beyond Medals: The Mission Continues

Winning the Nobel Peace Prize didn't slow Kailash down. In many ways, it gave him a louder megaphone. He continued to lead rescues, speak to governments and campaign across the globe.

He launched the 100 Million Campaign, calling on young people to stand up for the 100 million children worldwide still denied education and freedom. The campaign mobilised 6000 youngsters who volunteered to end violence against children and ensure education was accessible to every child around them. He addressed the United Nations, met world leaders and collaborated with global organisations to make child protection a central goal.

But no matter how big the stage, Kailash always returned to the ground. He visited villages, sat on dirt floors with children and asked them about their dreams.

*'Compassion is not just a feeling—
it is a force for change.'*

He believes that real change begins with everyday people. A teacher who refuses to turn a blind eye. A student who speaks up. A shopkeeper who says no to child labour. His message is that anyone can be a changemaker.

> **Did you know?**
>
> *As of today, Kailash Satyarthi and his team have helped rescue over 100,000 children from child labour, slavery and trafficking.*

He also founded the Bal Ashram Trust, a place where former child labourers are given shelter, education and skills training. Some of those rescued children are now teachers, lawyers and activists themselves.

Today, Kailash Satyarthi continues his work with the same fire that drove him as a boy with polished shoes and uncomfortable questions. He travels, speaks and organises—but always remains rooted in his mission.

In 2022, he was appointed as a United Nations Sustainable Development Goals Advocate, continuing his international work on education, justice and child safety. His journey reminds us that courage does not always roar.

Indian Roots, Global Impact

Born in India or of Indian ancestry, their ideas travelled across the globe and transformed human knowledge.

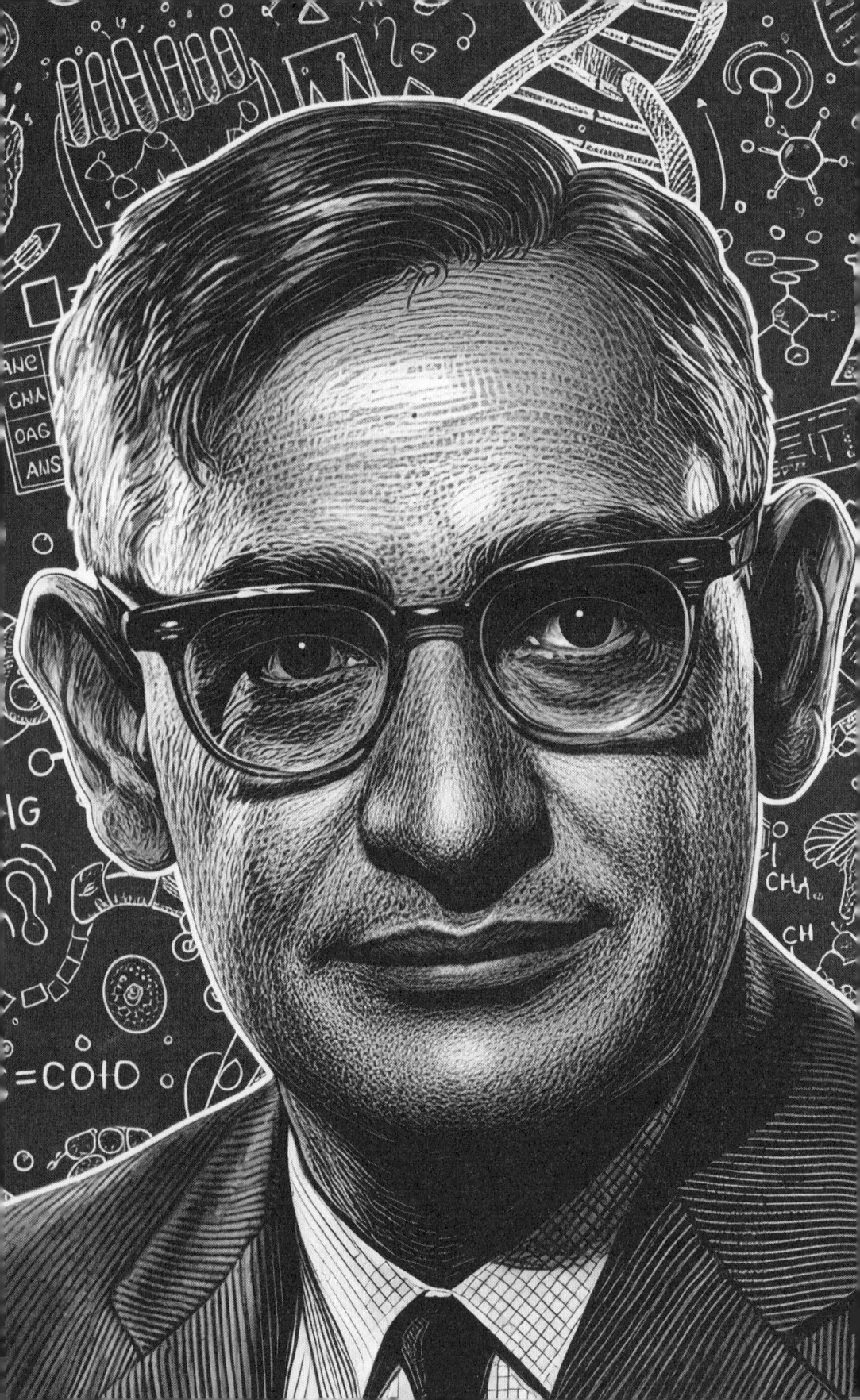

Har Gobind Khorana

 Born: 9 January 1922, Raipur, Multan, Punjab, British India (present-day Pakistan)

 Nobel Prize: Physiology or Medicine, 1968 (shared with Marshall W. Nirenberg and Robert W. Holley)

 Famous For: Revealing the genetic code that controls protein synthesis and creating the first synthetic gene

 Died: 9 November 2011, Concord, Massachusetts, USA

A Life of Curiosity and Quiet Determination

Har Gobind Khorana was born on 9 January 1922 in Raipur, a small village in Punjab, British India (now in Pakistan). His family was poor, but rich in values and determination. His father worked as a village clerk, earning very little, yet he made sure that all five of his children received an education. It was something almost unheard of in rural India at the time. He later recollected that theirs was practically the only literate family in the village.

The children studied under a tree in the village and shared the few books they had. Despite the simplicity of their surroundings, Khorana's curiosity burned bright. He was a quiet child, often drawn to the patterns of nature and the structure of language. This early curiosity would shape his lifelong interest in how life itself is coded. Khorana once said that he was lucky to have a father who believed strongly in education, even when there were no schools nearby.

He completed his early schooling in Multan, then studied at the University of the Punjab in Lahore, where he earned his bachelor's and master's degrees in chemistry. But opportunities in India were limited, and scholarships were rare. In 1945, fortune struck when he was awarded a scholarship to pursue a PhD at the University of Liverpool in England.

> **Did you know?**
>
> *Khorana travelled to England during the final years of World War II, and this was his first time ever leaving India. He carried with him only a small suitcase, and a burning desire to learn.*

Cracking the Language of Life

The 1950s and 60s were transformative decades in the field of genetics. Scientists had just discovered the structure of DNA, but many questions remained. Chief among them: how does DNA instruct cells to build proteins? Khorana joined this global scientific quest with characteristic rigour and humility.

In Canada, at the British Columbia Research Council, he studied the chemical structures of nucleic acids, the building blocks of DNA and RNA. But it was after he moved to the United States, to the University of Wisconsin, that his career reached new heights. There, he embarked on one of the most ambitious experiments of his time: synthesising a gene in the lab.

Working with fellow scientists Marshall Nirenberg and Robert Holley, Khorana helped unravel the genetic code—the system by the information inside our genes is turned into the proteins that allow every part of the body to work. Together, they showed how life's instructions are read and translated so that cells know exactly what to build.

> *'Biology is not just about observing. It is also about building,' Khorana said, explaining his approach to molecular biology.*

In a landmark achievement, he synthesised the first artificial gene in 1970. This experiment paved the way for modern genetic engineering, from insulin production to gene therapy. His work showed that life's code could not only be read, but also written.

Despite the magnitude of his discoveries, Khorana remained modest and often deflected praise to his colleagues. He once told his students, 'The only way to do science is to lose yourself in it.'

A Nobel Prize and a Moment of Global Recognition

In 1968, Har Gobind Khorana was awarded the Nobel Prize in Physiology or Medicine, alongside Nirenberg and Holley, for their collective work in interpreting the genetic code and its function in protein synthesis. For Khorana, the honour was not just a personal triumph but a symbol of what could be achieved through perseverance, collaboration and intellectual curiosity.

The Nobel Committee praised him for his work and called his synthetic gene experiments a 'revolution in biological chemistry.'

In his quiet manner, Khorana accepted the award and used the platform to speak about the role of education and opportunity. 'Science knows no country,' he always maintained. 'Its spark can begin in the most unlikely of places—even a small village with no school building.'

> **Did you know?**
>
> *Khorana was the first person of Indian origin to win a Nobel Prize in the field of physiology.*

His Nobel win made him a household name in India and abroad. Letters flooded in from students, researchers and well-wishers across the globe. Yet, he remained unchanged in his habits—waking early, walking to work and spending long hours in the lab. For him, the Nobel was not the end, but a milestone in a lifelong journey.

A Legacy That Continues to Inspire Generations

After his Nobel win, Khorana continued to push boundaries in science. In the 1970s, he joined the Massachusetts Institute of Technology (MIT), where he worked for the next three decades. There, he shifted his focus to membrane proteins and vision-related enzymes—the molecules in the eye that helps detect light.

Even as newer fields like genetic engineering and biotechnology emerged, Khorana's work provided the foundation. His methods of synthesising genes were precursors to techniques used today in gene therapy, synthetic biology and CRISPR—the gene modification technology.

But perhaps Khorana's most lasting legacy was his devotion to mentorship. He nurtured hundreds of students and researchers, encouraging them to be precise, bold and ethical. Many of them went on to become leading scientists in their own right.

> *'I have had a long and fulfilling life. But if I have contributed anything, it is because I was lucky to have good teachers, good colleagues and good students.'*

Khorana passed away in 2011 in Massachusetts at the age of 89. Yet his influence continues in labs, classrooms and research journals. His life story is often told in Indian schools as a symbol of how far education and determination can take someone, no matter their beginnings.

His legacy lives not in monuments or medals but in the countless young scientists who follow in his footsteps, curious and determined, just as he once was under that tree in Raipur.

In his memory, the Government of India and the Department of Biotechnology established the Khorana Program, which funds Indian students to undertake research internships in the United States.

■

Subrahmanyan Chandrasekhar

 Born: 19 October 1910, Lahore, Punjab, British India (now in Pakistan)

 Nobel Prize: Physics, 1983, for theoretical studies of the physical processes important to the structure and evolution of stars

 Famous For: Discovering the 'Chandrasekhar Limit,' which describes the maximum mass a white dwarf star can have

 Died: 21 August 1995, Chicago, Illinois, USA

The Boy Who Looked at the Stars

Subrahmanyan Chandrasekhar was born on 19 October 1910 in the warm city of Lahore, in British India (now in Pakistan). His family, part of a learned Tamil household, was filled with music, mathematics and books. His father was a government auditor who loved mathematics and music, while his mother encouraged reading and intellectual curiosity. Young Chandra, as everyone called him, was the nephew of the Nobel Laureate C.V. Raman. But even without that famous connection, Chandra was a bright star on his own.

From a very early age, Chandra loved to ask questions about how things worked. Why do stars shine? Why do they twinkle? What happens when they die? These were not easy questions, but Chandra never stopped wondering.

His parents made sure he received a strong education, first at home and then in school. Chandra was often seen buried in scientific journals or scribbling equations in the margins of his books. Even as a boy, he seemed to know his path was leading him towards a life in sciece.

'The pursuit of science has always seemed to me to be a search after truth.'

By the time he was a teenager, Chandra had published his first scientific paper in an Indian journal. This kind of achievement was nearly unheard of at the time. Still, he remained humble, eager to learn more.

> **Did you know?**
>
> *Chandra could recite long passages from classical Tamil poetry and also enjoyed Western classical music. His love for both science and the arts lasted his whole life.*

A Journey Across Oceans and Into the Unknown

At just 19 years of age, Chandra earned a scholarship to study at the University of Cambridge in England. The sea voyage from India to Britain took weeks. During that long trip, he read, thought and made calculations. And that's when he had an idea that would change the course of astrophysics.

He was thinking about white dwarf stars—stellar remnants left after a star burns out. At that time, it was believed that all stars ended their lifecycles as white dwarfs. But Chandra's calculations suggested something else entirely. He demonstrated that if a star were more than 1.4 times the mass of our Sun, it couldn't become a white dwarf. It would collapse under its own gravity. This limit, now famously known as the Chandrasekhar Limit, was groundbreaking.

When he presented this theory in 1935, many scientists rejected it, including Sir Arthur Eddington, a highly respected British astrophysicist. Eddington publicly dismissed the idea, which left Chandra embarrassed and disheartened. He later recalled the moment as one of the most painful in his career.

But Chandra did not give up.

'Science is a perception of the world around us. Science is a place where what you find in nature pleases you.'

Despite the criticism, he continued researching, refining his theories and publishing widely. He earned his PhD at Cambridge and, in 1937, moved to the United States to join the faculty at the University of Chicago. It would become his academic home for nearly 60 years.

> **Did you know?**
>
> *Chandra always carried a small notebook where he would jot down scientific thoughts—even while waiting in line or travelling on buses.*

The Chandrasekhar Limit and a Nobel Prize at Last

Chandra's prediction about the fate of massive stars eventually proved true. Scientists later confirmed that such stars collapse into neutron stars or black holes—concepts that revolutionised astrophysics. Although it took decades for the scientific world to accept his theories, Chandra lived long enough to see the recognition he so richly deserved.

In 1983, at the age of 73, Subrahmanyan Chandrasekhar was awarded the Nobel Prize in Physics. He shared it with William A. Fowler for their work on the structure and evolution of stars. The award citation specifically recognised his 'theoretical studies of the physical processes of importance to the structure and evolution of the stars.'

For Chandra, the prize was not just a personal honour, but also a recognition of the long and often lonely journey he had taken to uncover scientific truth. By then, he had mentored generations of students and had written over ten books and hundreds of papers.

He was known for his quiet voice, his precision in thought and his endless pursuit of excellence. His lectures were famously clear and thoughtful. His students adored him for his patience and brilliance.

> *'One must be intensely aware of the structure of the problem and see it from all sides.'*

Chandra was also unusual in his ability to switch fields. Every decade or so, he would move on to a new area—mathematical theory, stellar dynamics, general relativity, black holes and make foundational contributions in each.

Did you know?

Chandra never drove a car. He always walked to the University of Chicago or took the bus, enjoying the time to think quietly.

A Lasting Legacy That Still Lights Up the Sky

After winning the Nobel Prize, Chandra continued to work just as diligently. He never allowed himself to fall back on his laurels. Even in his later years, he could be found in his office, working through dense mathematical problems or preparing lectures. He remained humble, soft-spoken and gracious.

> **Did you know?**
>
> *Chandra once rewrote an entire 400-page manuscript because he felt the style wasn't clear enough—even though no one had asked him to do so.*

In 1990, NASA honoured him by naming one of its four 'Great Observatories' the Chandra X-ray Observatory. This powerful space telescope allows scientists to study the universe in X-ray light, helping them better understand black holes, neutron stars and distant galaxies. It remains one of NASA's most important scientific instruments.

Chandra also believed deeply in the beauty of science. He once described scientific discovery as 'an aesthetic experience,' comparing it to music or art. For him, science was not only about facts but also about elegance, clarity and wonder.

Though he passed away on 21 August 1995, Chandra's impact continues. His theories are still taught in classrooms, and his story inspires students across the world.

'The joy of science lies in uncovering the elegance of nature's design.'

Perhaps what made Chandra most extraordinary was not just his intellect, but his character. He never held grudges. He respected others' viewpoints. He was disciplined, precise and remarkably kind. His life shows that even the smallest questions or child-like musings like why stars shine, can lead to the biggest discoveries.

■

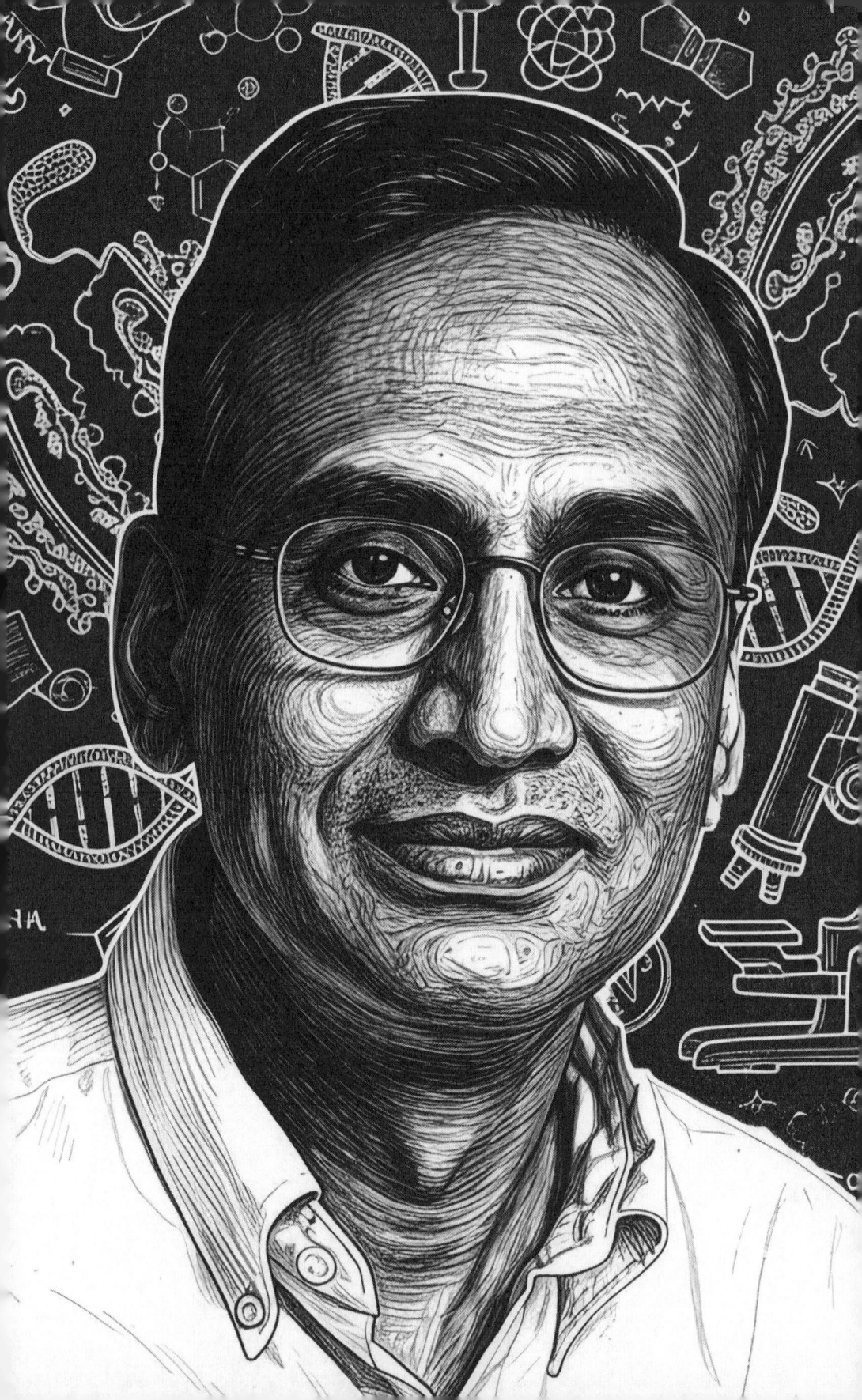

Venkatraman Ramakrishnan

 Born: 1952, Chidambaram, Tamil Nadu, India

 Nobel Prize: Chemistry, 2009 (shared with Thomas A. Steitz and Ada E. Yonath)

 Famous For: Groundbreaking work on the structure and function of the ribosome

Unveiling the Blueprint of Life

Venkatraman Ramakrishnan, known fondly as 'Venki,' was born on 1st July 1952, in Chidambaram, a small town in Tamil Nadu. His childhood was surrounded by books, science and the kind of open curiosity that often sparks future geniuses. His parents were both scientists. His father was a biochemist, and his mother was one of the first few women to earn a PhD in biochemistry in India. It was a home where science wasn't something distant or difficult—it was part of everyday life.

When Venki was a boy, the family moved to Baroda (now Vadodara) in Gujarat. There, he began to read voraciously. He was fascinated not only by science but by mathematics, literature and even philosophy. At the age of 16, he enrolled at Maharaja Sayajirao University to study physics. 'I was interested in understanding the laws that govern nature,' he later said.

Switching Paths and Following the Unknown

After completing his undergraduate studies in India, Venki moved to the United States in 1971 to pursue a PhD. But here's where the story takes a surprising turn: instead of continuing with physics, he switched to biology. It was a bold move that some found puzzling. Why leave behind the elegance of physics for the complexity of biology?

Venki himself admitted he didn't fully know what he was getting into. He pursued a PhD in Physics at Ohio University, but for his thesis, he focused on the behaviour of ribosomes—the tiny molecular machines that make proteins in all living cells. This decision would define the rest of his career.

> **Did you know?**
>
> *Venki once said that while he started as a physicist, he 'slowly defected' to biology because he wanted to work on problems that were 'less elegant, but more real.'*

After earning his PhD, Venki retrained as a postdoctoral researcher in biology at Yale University. It was not easy. He had to catch up on years of knowledge in molecular biology. But he was determined. He was captivated by the ribosome, a molecule so small it couldn't be seen under a normal microscope, yet so vital that without it, life couldn't exist.

'If you want to understand life, you have to understand how cells build themselves.'

He spent years working on visualising ribosomes, trying to understand their structure and function. This required mastering a technique called X-ray crystallography—a method that lets scientists take pictures of molecules by analysing how X-rays bounce off them.

Throughout the 1980s and 90s, Venki worked in labs across the United States and eventually settled at the MRC Laboratory of Molecular Biology in Cambridge, United Kingdom. There, he joined a small group of scientists determined to map the ribosome atom by atom.

It wasn't glamorous work. It involved painstaking effort, endless trial and error and an immense amount of patience. But it was the kind of work that could change the world.

> **Did you know?**
>
> *Venki was once rejected for a job at Cambridge early in his career. Years later, he became the President of the Royal Society in London—one of the oldest scientific institutions in the world.*

A Picture Worth a Nobel

In 2000, after decades of dedication, Venki and his team published a complete atomic map of a sub-unit of the ribosome. This was a groundbreaking moment in molecular biology. For the first time, scientists could see exactly how ribosomes help synthesise proteins—the very machinery of life.

This discovery had wide-reaching implications. It helped explain how antibiotics work and paved the way for new medicines. It also deepened our understanding of evolution, genetics and disease.

For this work, Venki was awarded the Nobel Prize in Chemistry in 2009. He shared the prize with two other scientists, Thomas A. Steitz and Ada Yonath, who were also working on mapping the ribosome.

'It was humbling,' he said, 'because I knew so many other brilliant people who had contributed to the field.'

Venki did not celebrate in grand fashion. He was famously modest and continued his work the next day, largely unchanged. He insisted that science was a team effort and that no great discovery came from a single person alone.

> **Did you know?**
>
> *When the Nobel committee first tried to reach Venki, he didn't answer the phone. He later said he thought it was a prank call!*

Championing Science and Curiosity

After receiving the Nobel Prize, Venki could have easily retired or moved into a quieter academic role. Instead, he used his position to speak out for science. In 2015, he became the President of the Royal Society in London—the first person of Indian origin to hold the post.

He spoke often about the importance of scientific literacy, the need to fund research and the danger of ignoring scientific facts in public policy. Venki also believed in encouraging young people to follow science—not just for jobs, but also, for the joy of asking questions.

'Science isn't just about knowledge,' he said. 'It's about learning how to think.'

Despite his success, Venki remained deeply grounded. He wrote a memoir titled *Gene Machine*, where he explained not just the science behind the ribosome but also the messy, human side of research: the competition, the failures and the doubts. He wanted young readers to know that scientists aren't all-knowing geniuses. They are simply people who are very good at not giving up.

He also used his platform to advocate for open science and diversity in research. He encouraged collaboration between countries and cultures and often reminded people that his own journey was shaped by opportunities that spanned two continents.

Today, Venkatraman Ramakrishnan is widely respected not only for his discoveries but also for his commitment to truth and reason. He continues to inspire new generations of scientists, especially those from countries like India, where resources are limited but dreams are not.

> **Did you know?**
>
> *In 2012, Venki was knighted by Queen Elizabeth II for his contributions to science.*

V. S. Naipaul

 Born: 17 August 1932, Chaguanas, Trinidad and Tobago

 Nobel Prize: Literature, 2001

 Famous For: Stories about people, countries and life after colonialism.

 Died: 11 August 2018, London, United Kingdom

 Citizenship: British (His family came from India, but he was born in the Caribbean island of Trinidad)

From the Sugarcane Fields to the City of Dreaming Spires

Vidiadhar Surajprasad Naipaul was born on 17 August 1932 in Chaguanas, Trinidad, into a family of Indian origin. His grandfather had arrived in the Caribbean as an indentured labourer who worked on sugar plantations, as part of the massive movement of Indians under British rule to colonies across the world. Naipaul grew up in a multigenerational Hindu household, steeped in rituals and the echoes of a homeland he had never seen.

> *'It is wrong to have an ideal view of the world. That's where the mischief starts. That's where everything starts to go wrong.'*

His father, Seepersad Naipaul, was a journalist who passed on both a love for writing and the struggles of the profession. 'He was not a good provider,' Naipaul would later write, 'but he gave me a sense of vocation.' Encouraged by his father's belief in literature, Vidiadhar devoured books in the public library, dreaming of escape and recognition.

At age 18, he won a government scholarship to study at Oxford University. It was a moment of great pride for his family, but also of tremendous personal challenge. In England, Naipaul experienced isolation and racism. 'No one knew where Trinidad was,' he recalled, 'and no one cared.' The loneliness at Oxford became the crucible in which his voice as a writer began to take shape.

> **Did you know?**
>
> *Naipaul suffered a nervous breakdown during his first year at Oxford. He once described walking around with suicidal thoughts, unsure of where he belonged.*

Carving a Voice with Unforgiving Precision

After graduating in 1953, Naipaul struggled to find his place in post-war Britain. He worked as a presenter for the BBC Caribbean Service, crafting short stories and essays in his spare hours. His first major success came in 1957 with *The Mystic Masseur,* a satirical novel about a Trinidadian man's rise to political power. It was funny, sharp and deeply rooted in colonial life.

> *'The world is what it is; men who are nothing, who allow themselves to become nothing, have no place in it.' – A Bend in the River*

But it was *A House for Mr Biswas* (1961), based on his father's life, that truly established Naipaul's place in literary history. The novel traced the struggles of an Indo-Trinidadian man trying to assert independence in a society that constantly belittled him. Mr Biswas's desire for 'a house of his own' became a metaphor for selfhood and dignity.

Naipaul's early novels often focused on small, post colonial societies—Trinidad, India, Guyana—where he unflinchingly dissected the confusions handed down across generations in colonial societies. His prose was exact, his observations often unsparing. Some critics admired his clarity, while others found him overly harsh or lacking compassion.

> **Did you know?**
>
> *Naipaul refused to romanticise India, calling it 'a country wounded by a thousand years of conquest.' This earned him both admiration and bitter criticism in India.*

Throughout the 1960s and 70s, Naipaul travelled widely, especially to India and Africa. Books such as *An Area of Darkness, India: A Wounded Civilisation* and *A Bend in the River* painted bleak pictures of nations struggling to define themselves in the shadow of colonialism. His books on India, in particular, stirred controversy. Some hailed them as brutally honest; others accused him of betraying his ancestral roots.

The Nobel Prize and the Unrelenting Eye

In 2001, V. S. Naipaul was awarded the Nobel Prize in Literature. The Swedish Academy praised him as a writer 'who has united perceptive narrative and incorruptible scrutiny in works that compel us to see the presence of suppressed histories.'

By the time of the Nobel, Naipaul had already won nearly every major literary prize in the English-speaking world—the Booker Prize in 1971 for *In a Free State*, the David Cohen Prize and a knighthood in 1990.

> *'The writer is the last person to be trusted with his own ideas. He should be suspicious of them.'*

For Naipaul, the Nobel was both a validation and an irony. Though long recognised for his talent, he had often stood at odds with the literary mainstream. He argued that writers should have 'no loyalties except to truth.' At the Nobel ceremony, he wore traditional black tie but gave a characteristically blunt speech. There were no flowery descriptions of literature as a balm for the soul. Instead, he spoke of suffering, survival and the necessity of clarity.

> **Did you know?**
>
> *Naipaul was only the second person of Indian origin to win the Nobel Prize in Literature, after Rabindranath Tagore in 1913.*

A Difficult Legacy: Fame, Controversy and Influence

Naipaul's later years were marked by a mix of reverence and disapproval. His works continued to provoke debate, particularly his essays on Islam and the developing world. In books like *Among the Believers* and *Beyond Belief*, he explored Islamic societies with a critical, even hostile eye, which many felt bordered on intolerance.

> *'What was past was fixed. But the future, though inevitable, was mutable, always changing.' – A House for Mr Biswas*

He was equally scrutinised for his personal life. Biographies revealed his complicated relationships with women, including emotional abuse of his first wife and a long affair with another woman. These revelations complicated public admiration for his writing.

Still, few disputed his literary influence. Writers such as Salman Rushdie, Chimamanda Ngozi Adichie and Zadie Smith acknowledged Naipaul's impact on post-colonial writing. His rigorous attention to detail, his elegant prose and his refusal to write comforting narratives forced a generation of writers to look harder at the realities of empire, migration and belonging.

> **Did you know?**
>
> *Naipaul never returned to live in Trinidad after leaving at 18, though he wrote about it throughout his life. He once said, 'Home for me is no longer a fixed place. It is ideas—and sometimes people.'*

Naipaul passed away on 11 August 2018 in London. His death marked the end of a long, luminous literary journey. He had written over thirty books, covering continents, centuries and complexities of human existence.

Nobel Work on Indian Soil

Discoveries shaped by India's land, labs and lived realities—breakthroughs that echoed worldwide.

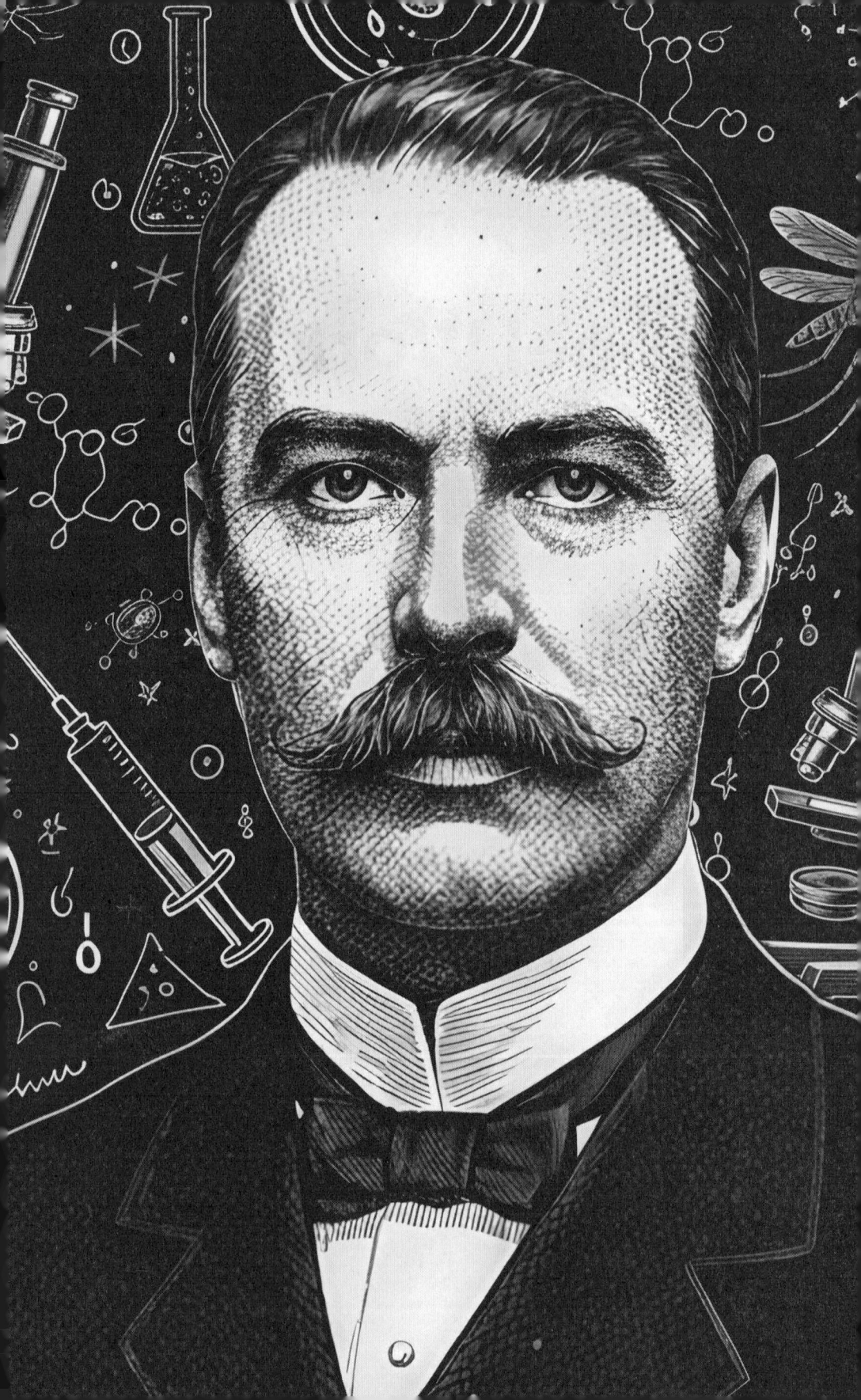

Ronald Ross

 Born: 13 May 1857, Almora, British India (now in Uttarakhand, India)

 Nobel Prize: Physiology or Medicine, 1902

 Famous For: Discovering that malaria is transmitted by mosquitoes

 Died: 18 January 1936, London, United Kingdom

 Citizenship: British citizen, born and educated partly in colonial India where he also conducted groundbreaking research

Breaking the Malaria Code

Ronald Ross was born to a Scottish family in the quiet Himalayan town of Almora, nestled in the hills of what is now Uttarakhand, India. His father Campbell Claye Grant Ross was a general in the British Indian Army, who encouraged discipline and study, while his mother Matilda Charlotte Elderton filled their home with books and music. From a young age, Ronald loved to sketch, write poetry and tinker with puzzles. But like many English children growing up in India during the British Raj, the country's natural world left young Ronald absorbed.

He was fascinated by the buzzing insects and chirping birds around him. 'Nature speaks to those who listen,' he would later write, a line that reflected his lifelong curiosity.

When he was eight, Ronald was sent to England for schooling, like many children of British officers. He missed India terribly. The grey skies of England felt dull compared to the vibrant landscapes of his childhood. Though he showed more interest in poetry and mathematics than in biology, his father persuaded him to study medicine.

> **Did you know?**
>
> *Ronald Ross was also a writer and published several volumes of poetry, plays and fiction throughout his life.*

After qualifying as a doctor in 1881, Ross returned to India with the Indian Medical Service. He was stationed in cities like Madras, Bangalore and Secunderabad. While the routine work of examining patients was demanding, Ross was not content with treating illnesses. He wanted to understand them, to go to their very roots.

The Mosquito, the Parasite and a Patient Named Hussain Khan

At that time, malaria was one of the deadliest diseases in the world. Millions were falling ill each year, especially in tropical countries like India. But no one truly knew how it spread. Some believed it came from 'bad air' in swamps. Others blamed poor sanitation. The idea that it could be passed from mosquitoes to humans was still just a hypothesis.

Ross was deeply influenced by the work of Charles Louis Alphonse Laveran, a French doctor who had discovered parasites in the blood of malaria patients. Ross began to study the blood of malaria victims in India, searching for patterns.

One of his turning points came in 1897 when a soldier named Hussain Khan was brought to him in Secunderabad, suffering from a violent fever. Ross examined Khan's blood and noticed strange crescent-shaped parasites. He dissected mosquitoes that had fed on the soldier and found the same parasites developing in the insect's gut.

On 20 August 1897, Ross made the breakthrough that would define his career: he demonstrated that the malaria parasite could develop inside a mosquito, proving that mosquitoes were responsible for transmitting the disease. It was the *Anopheles* mosquito in particular that carried the parasite from person to person.

'This day I made a great discovery,' Ross wrote in his diary. 'I found the parasites in the stomach of the mosquito. The discovery is perhaps the greatest I have made yet.'

> **Did you know?**
>
> *In India, 20 August is celebrated as Mosquito Day in honour of Ross's discovery.*

Ross's work did not stop with this discovery. He went on to show how malaria could be prevented by controlling mosquito populations. He encouraged the use of mosquito nets, draining swamps and clearing stagnant water—practices that are still used in malaria control today.

Despite his groundbreaking discovery, Ross's research was not always appreciated at the time. He had limited funding, and he faced opposition from senior doctors who did not believe in his theories. Yet he remained determined, often writing and sketching deep into the night.

A Nobel Prize and a World That Took Notice

In 1902, Ronald Ross received the Nobel Prize in Physiology or Medicine, becoming the first British citizen and the first person born in India to win a Nobel. He was honoured for 'his work on malaria, by which he has shown how it enters the organism,' a discovery that changed medicine forever.

> *'Science is the searchlight of truth. It lights up the path to health, hope and progress.'*

The Nobel Prize brought Ross international recognition. He was knighted by King George V and became a fellow of the Royal Society. He also became a professor of tropical medicine at the University of Liverpool, where he trained new doctors and continued his research.

But fame did not soften Ross's edge. He often clashed with colleagues, especially when they took credit for work he felt was his own. He engaged in a long and bitter dispute with Giovanni Battista Grassi, an Italian scientist who had also been researching malaria transmission. Ross accused Grassi of downplaying his contribution.

Despite the controversies, Ross's scientific contributions were undeniable. His discovery helped launch the field of tropical medicine and paved the way for future work on mosquito-borne illnesses such as dengue, chikungunya and Zika virus.

> **Did you know?**
>
> *Ross insisted on spelling his name in capital letters, RONALD ROSS, in many of his later papers and letters, to ensure proper credit.*

Beyond the Lab: A Legacy of Science, Service and Song

After his Nobel Prize win, Ross continued to travel widely, from West Africa to the Suez Canal, studying malaria outbreaks and advising on how to prevent them. He also worked during First World War, serving as a consultant on malaria for the British Army.

In later life, Ross became increasingly passionate about public health and education. He believed that scientific research should benefit the poorest, not just the privileged. He urged governments to fund more research and invest in sanitation and mosquito control.

Ross also returned to writing. He published scientific papers, novels, plays and even poems about science and discovery. In one of his poems, *The Child of the Future*, he wrote:

> *'Science, thou fair white child,*
> *Born of the brain of man,*
> *Speeding on tireless wings*
> *Toward the infinite plan.'*

'Science is the Differential Calculus of the mind. Art is the Integral Calculus; they may be beautiful when apart, but are greatest only when combined,' he'd say.'

Though Ross's final years were spent in England, his heart remained tied to India. He died in London in 1932 at the age of 75, but his ashes were interred at Putney Vale Cemetery with a plaque honouring his service to humanity.

Did you know?

Ronald Ross's discovery helped save an estimated 7 million lives during the Second World War alone, thanks to mosquito control in army camps and tropical battlefields.

Today, Ronald Ross is remembered as one of the greatest medical pioneers of all time. His name lives on in hospitals, research centres and awards, and his discovery continues to protect lives every day in countries across the globe.

Rudyard Kipling

 Born: 30 December 1865, Bombay (now Mumbai), British India

 Nobel Prize: Literature, 1907 (youngest recipient at the time)

 Famous For: Author of *The Jungle Book*, *Kim* and poems like *If*; known for vivid storytelling and portrayal of colonial India

 Died: 18 January 1936, London, United Kingdom

 Citizenship: British citizen, born and raised in British India

The Wordsmith Between Worlds

Born on 30 December 1865 in Bombay, Rudyard Kipling's earliest memories were filled with colour, language and the layered texture of Indian life. His father, John Lockwood Kipling, was a British professor of architectural sculpture, and his mother, Alice MacDonald, came from a cultured English family. Though they were part of the British colonial elite, the Kipling household was open to local traditions, and young Rudyard was exposed to Hindu tales, Urdu lullabies and bustling Indian streets—sights and sounds that would shape his imagination for decades to come..

At the age of six, however, Kipling's idyllic Indian childhood was abruptly halted. He and his sister were sent to England to live with a foster family in Southsea, as was common practice among colonial families. The years he spent in that strict and often cruel household—which he called the 'House of Desolation'—marked a stark contrast to his early freedom and warmth in India.

'There were no kisses, or kind words, or smiles… I had never heard of hell, so I was introduced to it in all its terrors,' Kipling later wrote of the experience.

> **Did you know?**
>
> *Kipling's unusual name came from Rudyard Lake in Staffordshire, where his parents had met and fallen in love.*

The trauma of his English childhood left an indelible mark on Kipling, but it also awakened in him a deep sensitivity and a longing for the storytelling warmth of India. He found solace in reading, especially the works of Charles Dickens, and later channelled his inner turmoil into fiction filled with both wonder and shadow.

The Journalist Who Became a Literary Giant

Returning to India at age 16, Kipling began work as a journalist for the *Civil and Military Gazette* in Lahore. The job gave him the opportunity to explore the vastness of the Indian subcontinent, from army outposts to railway stations and dusty towns. His observations quickly turned into short stories and poems, many of which were published in small volumes. His first major breakthrough came in 1888 with the publication of *Plain Tales from the Hills*.

His sharp storytelling and gift for dialogue caught the attention of the British public. By the time he returned to England in 1889, Kipling was already being hailed as a rising literary star. In 1892, Kipling married Caroline Balestier and settled in Vermont, USA, where he wrote *The Jungle Book*. Though their time in America was short-lived due to family disputes and cultural differences, it was a fruitful period for his writing. Over the next decade, he released some of his most celebrated works, including *The Jungle Book* (1894), *The Second Jungle Book* (1895) and *Kim* (1901). These stories wove together adventure, moral lessons and a deep engagement, if somewhat romanticised, with Indian society.

'He writes books I can read,' said Theodore Roosevelt, who admired Kipling for his direct style and masculine ethos.

Despite his accolades as one of the most creative writers of his time, some of his political viewpoints were deeply objectionable. Kipling coined the term 'white man's burden' in a poem of the same name, which became controversial for its imperial overtones. The poem was addressed to the United States, urging it to take on colonial responsibilities in the Philippines.

Despite criticism of his perceived support of empire, Kipling's literary prowess was undeniable. His rhythmic poetry, such as *If, Gunga Din* and *The Ballad of East and West*, cemented his status as a master wordsmith.

The Nobel Laureate and the Height of Fame

In 1907, Rudyard Kipling became the first English-language writer—and the youngest recipient at the time—to win the Nobel Prize in Literature. The Swedish Academy praised him for 'the power of observation, originality of imagination, virility of ideas and remarkable talent for narration which characterise the creations of this world-famous author.'

The honour reflected his towering presence in global literature. Kipling was now a household name, read in classrooms and quoted by statesmen. His works were translated into multiple languages, and children across continents were enchanted by Mowgli, Bagheera and Baloo. Yet fame brought scrutiny.

> **Did you know?**
>
> ***Kipling was offered both a knighthood and the position of British Poet Laureate, but he declined both.***

The Nobel Prize marked both a peak and a turning point in his life. As the world changed—with growing anti-colonial sentiment, the horrors of the First World War and shifting literary styles—Kipling's imperial sympathies were increasingly questioned.

Tragically, the First World War dealt Kipling a devastating blow. His only son, John, was killed in battle at the age of 18. Kipling had used his influence to secure John a commission despite his poor eyesight. For the rest of his life, he carried the weight of that decision.

> *'If any question why we died,*
> *Tell them, because our fathers lied,'*
> *Kipling wrote later, reflecting the anguish and regret he felt.*

Shadows, Legacy and the Echo of His Voice

In his later years, Kipling continued to write, though with a darker, more sombre tone. His war poems and stories revealed a man disillusioned by violence and death. He remained active in public life, serving on the Imperial War Graves Commission and helping to shape remembrance culture in Britain.

Kipling died on 18 January 1936 at the age of 70. He was buried in Westminster Abbey, close to the graves of Charles Dickens and Thomas Hardy—a fitting resting place for one of English literature's most influential figures.

> **Did you know?**
>
> ***Though Kipling's works are sometimes viewed through a political lens, his children's stories have endured for their timeless themes of courage, belonging and friendship.***

His legacy remains complex. Critics have long debated the colonial attitudes in his work. Others argue that Kipling was a nuanced observer of empire, capable of both admiration and critique. Indeed, *Kim*, his most mature novel, presents a layered, multicultural view of India that is neither wholly romanticised nor simplistic.

'For the strength of the Pack is the Wolf, and the strength of the Wolf is the Pack.' - The Jungle Book

Today, Kipling's writing remains a staple in school curricula and libraries. From adventure stories to reflective poetry, his words continue to ignite the imagination of readers. Museums, films and stage adaptations keep his characters alive. Whether celebrated or critiqued, Kipling's voice is one that refuses to fade.

∎

Laureates Who Call India Home

Global voices whose life, work or spiritual journey found refuge, purpose and resonance in India.

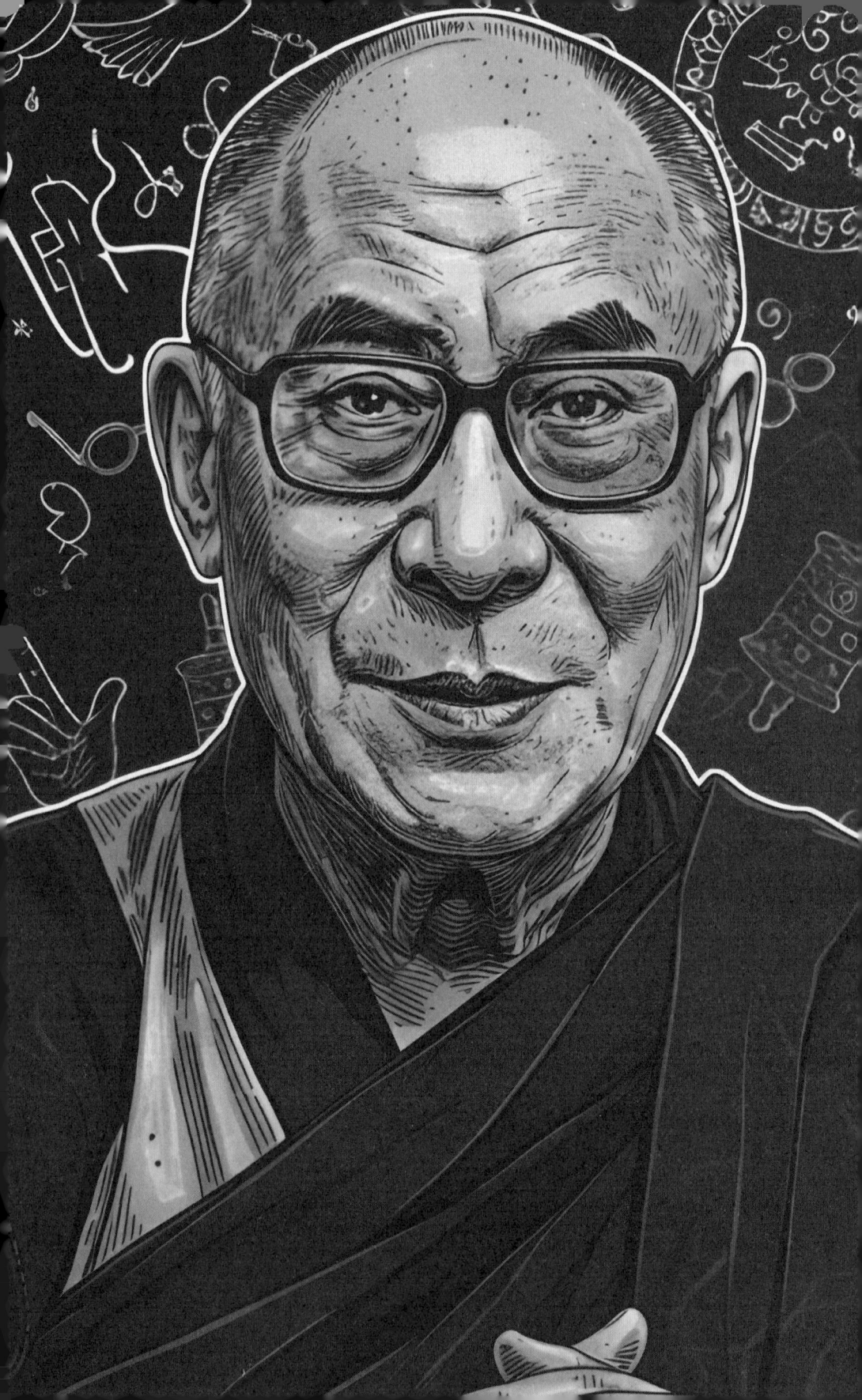

14th Dalai Lama

 Born: 6 July 1935, Taktser, Amdo, Tibet (now in Qinghai, China)

 Nobel Prize: Peace, 1989

 Famous For: Promoting non-violence, human rights, compassion and the peaceful struggle for Tibetan autonomy

 Citizenship: Stateless (Tibetan by heritage, residing in India as a refugee since 1959)

A Monk Across Borders

On 6 July 1935, in the remote village of Taktser in northeastern Tibet, a baby boy named Lhamo Thondup was born to a humble farming family. The village was nestled in the Amdo province, surrounded by snow-covered mountains and monasteries. Life was simple and deeply spiritual. No one could have predicted that this child would become the Dalai Lama—the highest spiritual leader of Tibetan Buddhism, and one of the most influential voices for peace in the twentieth and twenty-first centuries.

At the age of two, Buddhist monks arrived in Taktser, following ancient signs and visions pointing them to the next reincarnation of the Dalai Lama, Tibet's spiritual and political leader. According to Tibetan Buddhist belief, the Dalai Lama is the reincarnation of Avalokiteshvara, the Bodhisattva of compassion (a reincarnation of Buddha). After a series of tests, including identifying items belonging to the previous Dalai Lama, the boy was declared the 14th Dalai Lama.

He was soon taken to Lhasa, the capital of Tibet, to begin his monastic education in the Potala Palace. There he was renamed Tenzin Gyatso. His education covered Buddhist philosophy, logic, metaphysics and Sanskrit, all of which he mastered with diligence and humility.

> *'The true hero is one who conquers his own anger and hatred.'*

Forced to Lead: A Young Monk Faces Invasion and Exile

At just fifteen years old, the Dalai Lama was thrust into a position of power he never expected so soon. In 1950, the Chinese government invaded Tibet, claiming it as part of China. The young spiritual leader was forced to step into political leadership to try and negotiate peace. For nearly a decade, he attempted dialogue with Chinese authorities. However, by 1959, the situation had worsened, and the Tibetan people rose in a mass protest in Lhasa, which led to a brutal crackdown.

Fearing for his life and the safety of his people, the Dalai Lama disguised himself as a soldier and fled on horseback across the Himalayas. After a grueling two-week journey through treacherous terrains, he reached India and was granted asylum by Prime Minister Jawaharlal Nehru.

Settling in Dharamshala, a quiet hill town in Himachal Pradesh, the Dalai Lama established the Tibetan Government-in-Exile. His days in India were marked by hardship, yet also fueled by hope. Thousands of Tibetan refugees followed him. He dedicated his time to preserving Tibetan culture, religion and language and teaching his people the power of non-violence.

Did you know?

The Indian town of Dharamshala is sometimes called 'Little Lhasa' because it houses the Tibetan parliament-in-exile and the Central Tibetan Administration.

The Peace Prize for a Message of Non-Violence

By the 1980s, the Dalai Lama had become a global figure. He travelled the world, spreading messages of compassion, interfaith harmony and peaceful resistance. Despite losing his homeland, he refused to endorse violence. Instead, he sought meaningful dialogue, even with those he disagreed with. This unique approach caught the attention of global leaders and peace organisations.

'Love and compassion are necessities, not luxuries. Without them, humanity cannot survive.'

In 1989, he was awarded the Nobel Peace Prize for his consistent non-violent struggle for the liberation of Tibet and for his concern for global environmental problems. The award was especially symbolic as it came shortly after the Tiananmen Square protests in China, where peaceful demonstrators had been met with violence. The Nobel Committee honoured him for showing that peace could be won without weapons.

In his acceptance speech, the Dalai Lama said, 'Peace does not mean the absence of violence. Peace means the presence of compassion.'

The Nobel Prize gave the Tibetan cause global recognition, but the Dalai Lama used it to highlight broader issues like religious tolerance, human rights and the ethical responsibility of humanity.

Did you know?

The Dalai Lama is the first Nobel Peace Prize laureate to be recognised for advocating environmental responsibility as part of global peace.

A Global Icon of Peace, Humour and Humility

Even decades after his exile, the Dalai Lama continues to be one of the most beloved spiritual leaders in the world. Although he stepped down from political leadership in 2011, handing over his role to an elected leader, he remains the spiritual head of Tibetan Buddhism. He travels across continents, meeting schoolchildren, scientists, religious leaders and heads of state, always spreading his message of compassion.

> **Did you know?**
>
> *The Dalai Lama had a fascination for science even as a young monk. He later became the first Dalai Lama to collaborate with scientists and promote the dialogue between Buddhism and modern physics.*

He's known for his infectious laugh, simple robes and deep wisdom. Despite meeting royalty and presidents, he often introduces himself by saying, 'I am just a simple Buddhist monk.' His teachings encourage people to look inward for peace and to live ethically and mindfully.

He has authored over 100 books on diverse topics such as compassion, happiness, science, ethics and mindfulness. Some of his best-known works include *The Art of Happiness* and *The Book of Joy*.

> **Did you know?**
>
> *In 2007, the United States Congress awarded the Dalai Lama its highest civilian honour, the Congressional Gold Medal.*

Though he is now in his late eighties, the Dalai Lama remains active. His legacy is not just about Tibet, but also focused on teaching the world that true strength lies in gentleness, and that peace begins with individual hearts.

■